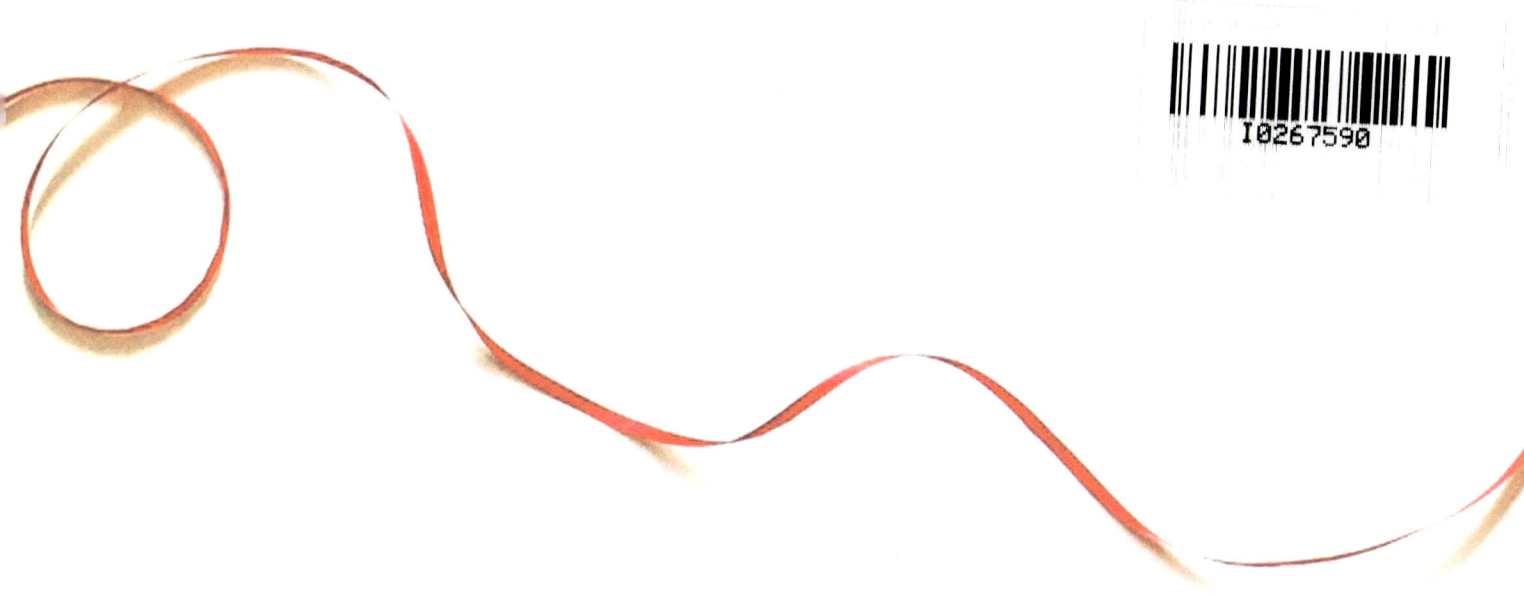

Dedicated to all those who helped me grow the most and whose growth I've been a part of.

Copyright © Shirley Harvey 2017
All rights reserved. No part of this book may be reproduced, transmitted, or stored in an information retrieval system in any form or by any means, graphic, electronic, or mechanical, including photocopying, taping, and recording, without prior written permission from the publisher.

First edition 2017
ISBN 978-1-7750646-3-3
Published by Animal Publications in a magical place called Shirley World.
www.shirleyharvey.com

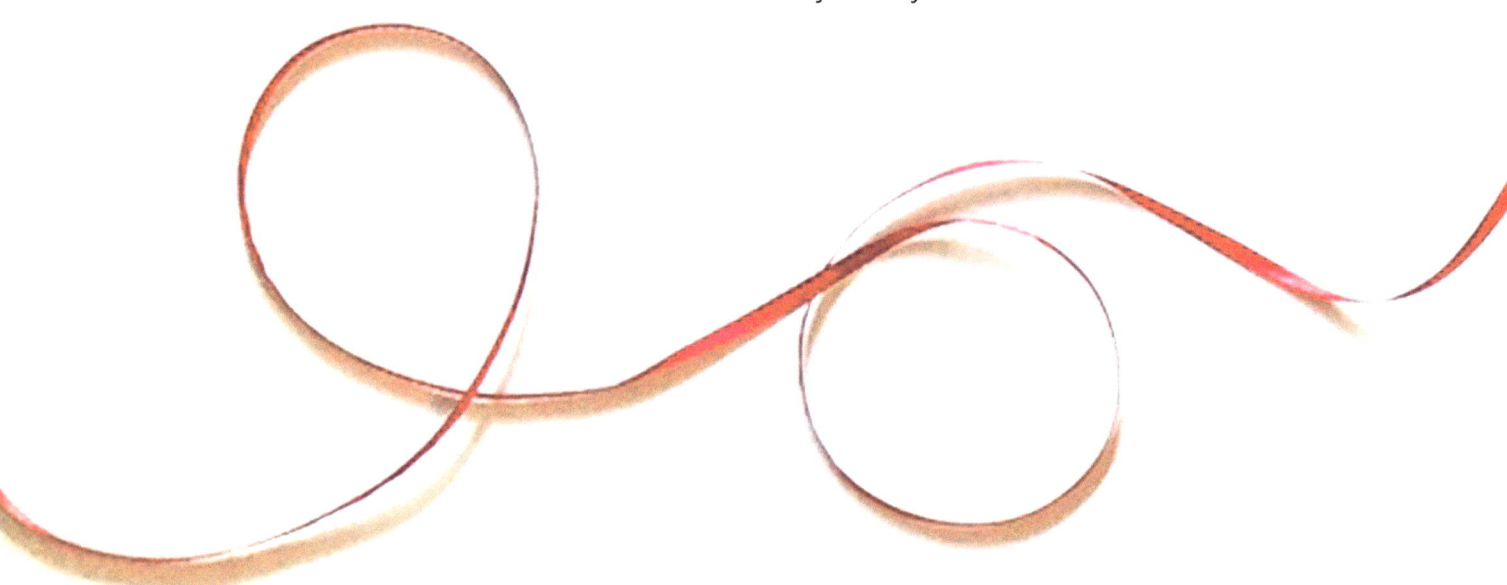

Written and Illustrated by Shirley Harvey

I feel I'm bursting right out of my skin.
There's something inside that's growing within,
But there isn't the space,
There isn't a place
For this thing that's inside me
To spread and be free.

So now I know what I'm going to do,
I'm done with the clutter, I'm done, I'm through.
I'm making room
For this thing to bloom
Because in my heart I know

It needs some space to grOW.

I know it's not easy, letting go,
Of friends, belongings, places I know.
But strength I will find,
I will always be kind
And say thank you with grace
As I let go and make space.

She dreamt of things she'd never been,
She dreamt of things she'd never seen,
She dreamt of things, good and bad,
Beautiful, ugly, happy and sad.
She dreamt of things she wanted to do,
Wonderful things she had to pursue.

There once was a fish with a great big dream

Of oceans wide and lands unseen.

He would spend all day

In imaginative play,

Fighting sea monsters and the odd sardine.

Debra the Zebra truly believed

She was one of a kind, a magical breed.

Whatever they thought of her,

She chose not to mind,

She believed she was a unicorn,

One of a kind.

If you are far too scared to try,

To spread your wings and learn to fly,

The chances are incredibly high

That this is the thing you were born to do,

And this is the thing that will make you You.

The hardest thing for you to do,
When you want to do something new,
Is pluck up the courage within your heart,
Take a leap of faith and simply start.

It was going to be difficult, he knew it would be,

He'd already fallen and hurt his knee.

The wheels whirled too fast,

His legs followed suit,

And to think he thought it would be a hoot,

But he knew he'd regret it if he didn't try,

And at least it could be a fun way to die!

"Ouch!" That hurt his trunk and his pride.

There was nowhere on earth for his shame to hide.

With his face in the dirt and his butt in the air,

He wanted to shout, "This just isn't fair!"

But he knew that with each spectacular fail,

If he got back in the saddle, readjusted his tail,

He'd definitely improve and may even succeed

In being a unicyclist, guaranteed.

Bear sat on a rock one day

And reflected he needed a different way,

A different way to work things out,

A different way to remove the doubt.

Measure up,

Baby duck,

And then you will see

By trusting yourself,

How great you can be.

A very silly thing to do

Is to keep repeating the same things through.

If things aren't working, it's time for a change,

Time to adjust, try something strange.

If at first your dreams resist,

Never give up, you must persist.

With one step at a time and a lot of smiles,

You'll soon be traversing many miles.

And then one day
New friends come our way,
Offering a paw
Or even a claw,
Helping us up,
Refilling our cup
Full of kindness and love,
Divine help from above.

The saddest fate for a dream to befall

Is not to finish the project at all,

To leave it unfinished, on the 'one day' list,

The power of finishing can't be dismissed.

So, pull up your breeches

And go with the flow,

You will be glad that you did,

It allowed you to grOW.

Grow fourth into your world
x

Shirley is an artist, writer, entrepreneur and mother with a sweet and whimsical take on the world.

Using her unique style of painting and writing, and her team of trusted animal friends, she brings to light the finer qualities and quirks of what it means to be human with humour and grace.

www.shirleyharvey.com